Pastoral Care: Principles And Practices

Oscar MONONO

Copyright © 2025 Oscar MONONO

No part of this book may be reproduced, distributed, or transmitted in any form or by any means, including photocopying, recording, or other electronic or mechanical methods, without the prior written permission of the publisher and the author, except in the case of brief quotations used in reviews or certain other non-commercial uses permitted by copyright law.

Publisher: Upway Books
Authors: Oscar MONONO
Title: Pastoral Care: Principles And Practices
ISBN: 978-1-917916-25-7
Cover: www.canva.com

This book is a work of non-fiction. The information it contains is based on the author's research, experience, and knowledge at the time of publication. The publisher and authors have made every effort to ensure the accuracy and reliability of the information provided, but assume no responsibility for any errors, omissions, or differing interpretations of the subject matter. This publication is not intended to replace professional advice or consultation. Readers are encouraged to seek professional guidance where appropriate.

contact@upwaybooks.com
www.upwaybooks.com

Dedication

This book is dedicated to my wife: Eposi Sylvie Monono. I equally dedicate this book to Grace Theological Seminary(GTS).

Acknowledgment

I will like to thank the efforts of five persons whose supports and contributions made this project a reality. These persons are; Rev. Dr. Joeys Itue Motomby, Rev.Dr. Rudolph kwanue, Rev.Dr. Saleh Johnathan, Dr. Fritz Mbua, and My colleagues in Grace Theological Seminary, USA.

Foreword

This book titled *"Pastoral care: Principles and Practices"* written by **Dr. Oscar Monono** has addressed historical, religious and professional concepts of the caregiving profession. Caregiving is not just visiting and showing empathy. It encompasses a comprehensive attention to caregiving environment and the clients. The book gives us clear qualities, and principles in the caregiving profession. This book went further to demonstrate the new testament model of caregiving. Jesus and the apostles are models in the caregiving profession. This book is structured in a way that ease understanding. It has short practical exercises. It is educational in presentation. It is presented in a manner that could be used by students, pastoral caregivers, ministers of the gospel, faith-based organizations to increase capacity, ability and attitude in their caregiving profession.

I recommend this book in various capacities and jurisdictions within which such knowledge, skills and career is required.

Dr. Magnus Richardson PhD.

grimsinfos21@gmail.com

Contents

CHAPTER ONE: INTRODUCTION 7

CHAPTER TWO: Pastoral Care Profession 39

CHAPTER THREE: Biblical Models of Pastoral Care and Counseling 62

CHAPTER ONE

INTRODUCTION

1.0 Introduction

pastoral care refers to emotional, social and spiritual support. The term is considered inclusive of distinctly non-religious forms of support, as well as support for people from religious communities.

Pastoral care as a contemporary term is distinguished from traditional pastoral ministry, which is primarily Christian and tied to Christian beliefs. Institutional pastoral care departments in Europe are increasingly multi-faith and inclusive of non-religious, humanist approaches to providing support and comfort.

Just as the theory and philosophy behind modern pastoral care are not dependent on any one set of beliefs or traditions, pastoral care itself is guided by a broad framework. This involves personal support and outreach and is rooted in a practice of relating with the inner world of individuals from all walks of life.

Pastoral care is usually provided in the form of the practitioner and client sitting with each other and the client shares personal details while the practitioner keeps it private and offers guidance and counsel.

1.1. Christianity

Definition

Pastoral Care is a Christian approach to improve mental distress and has been practiced since the formation of the Christian Church. By offering guidance and counsel, it is an easy and often preferred contact point for religious people seeking help with psychological problems or personal issues. The model for pastoral care is based on the stories about how Jesus was healing people.

In the early church the term *'Poimenic'* was used to describe this task of soul care. In the New Testament, the interactions that are described with the term "pastoral care" are also described with ***Paraklesis*** which broadly means "accompaniment", "encouragement", "admonition" and "consolation" (e.g. Rom 12,8; Phil 2,1; 1 Tim 4,13; 1 Thes 5,14).

Pastoral care occurs in various contexts, including congregations, hospital chaplaincy, crisis intervention, prison chaplaincy, psychiatry, telephone helplines, counseling centers, senior care facilities, disability work, hospices, end-of-life care, grief support, and more.

The term pastoral ministry relates to shepherds and their role caring for sheep. Christians were the first to adopt the term for metaphorical usage, although many religions and non-religious traditions place an emphasis on care and social responsibility. In the West, pastoral ministry has since expanded into pastoral care embracing many different religions and non-religious beliefs.

The Bible does not explicitly define the role of a pastor but associates it with teaching. Pastoral ministry involves shepherding the flock. Shepherding involves protection, tending to needs, strengthening the weak, encouragement, feeding the flock, making provision, shielding, refreshing, restoring, leading by example to move people on in their pursuit of holiness, comforting, guiding (Ps 78: 52; 23).

1.2. History of pastoral care and counseling

In the ancient church, pastoral care primarily revolved around the Christian's struggle against sin, which jeopardized their ultimate salvation. The theologians Clement of Alexandria, Origen and Eusebius of Caesarea mainly understood this as the concern of individuals for their own souls. Increasingly, the role of pastoral caregivers was seen as assisting individual Christians in this endeavor. The first pastoral movement emerged among the Desert Fathers, who were often visited by Christians seeking advice; however, this was not yet referred to as pastoral care. Similarly, the early monastic-like communities served as such pastoral care centers. The letters of Basil of Ancyra, Gregory of Nazianzus, and John Chrysostom contain numerous examples of pastoral counsel; the term "pastoral care" shifted towards a concern for the souls of others. At the transition to the Middle Ages, Gregory the Great composed the "Liber Regulae Pastoris", directed towards the Pope, one of the most influential books on pastoral care (cura) ever written.

During the Middle Ages, pastoral care was closely tied to the practice of the sacrament of penance, which included confession of sins, making amends, and absolution by the priest. Against the often mechanized routine, particularly from the monastic tradition, efforts were made to address this, such as by Bernard of Clairvaux. The Latin term "cura animarum" (care of souls) emerged as the proper responsibility of the bishop as the pastor responsible for individual Christians, which he usually delegated to a priest, typically the parish priest. In this sense of religion" is also used in today's canon law of the Roman Catholic Church.

Among the Reformers, the emphasis shifted from the focus on sin to the emphasis on God's forgiveness and comfort, particularly evident in the works of Martin Luther and Heinrich Bullinger. In many cases, however, church discipline soon replaced pastoral care.

In the 19th century, the Protestant theologian Friedrich Schleiermacher established Practical Theology. He emphasized that pastoral care should strengthen the freedom and autonomy of individual members within a congregation. As early as 1777, the field of Pastoral Theology was introduced into the curriculum of the University of Vienna (Austria) under Franz Stephan Rautenstrauch, and was taught in the national language rather than Latin. In Germany, it was further developed and disseminated primarily by Johann Michael Sailer, and is considered a precursor to modern pastoral care.

In the United States, Anton Theo Phil, one of the key figures in the American pastoral care movement, developed the concept of "Clinical Pastoral Training" in the 1920s. This concept integrated pastoral care, psychology, and education.

In the mid-1960s, the pastoral care movement spread to Germany through the Netherlands, leading to the development of Pastoral Psychology. In the theology of the regional churches, pastoral care with a focus on pastoral psychology remains a standard practice to this day.

Activity 1.1

1. Define pastoral care from three backgrounds------------------------------------
----

----

2. Explain the traditional history of pastoral care------------------------------------
----

1.3. Modern Context

The field of pastoral care is nowadays very specialized. Browning (1993) divided Christian care giving practices into three different categories which are pastoral care, pastoral counseling, and pastoral psychotherapy. This distinction can still be found nowadays, especially in written English papers. According to this definition, pastoral care describes the general work of the clergy of taking care of the people in their community. This comprises funerals, hospital visits, birthday visits or dialogues that do not focus only on a specific problem.

Nowadays, there exist many approaches to pastoral care which vary according to their religious denomination. Many protestant Christian approaches to pastoral care include contemporary psychological knowledge, which is reflected in the training of pastoral care practitioners. For example, in Germany, the distinctions and the curricula of the different pastoral care training approaches, are provided by the German Society for Pastoral Psychology (Deutsche, Pastoral psychology). The five approaches are clinical pastoral care, the group-organization-system approach (Group-Organization, System), the Gestalt and psychodrama approach (Gestalt und Psychodrama), the person-centric approach (Person centered) and the depth psychology approach.

1.4. Humanist and non-Religious

Humanist groups, which act on behalf of non-religious people, have developed pastoral care offerings in response to growing demand for the provision of like-minded support from populations undergoing rapid secularization, such as the UK. Humanists UK, for example, manages the Non-Religious Pastoral Support Network, a network of trained and accredited volunteers and professionals who operate throughout prisons, hospitals, and universities in the UK. The terms pastoral care and pastoral support are preferred because these sound less religious than terms such as chaplaincy. Surveys have shown that more than two thirds of patients support non-religious pastoral care being available in British institutions. Similar offerings are available from humanist groups around Europe and North America.

1.5. Pastoral care in Roman Catholicism, Protestantism and other Christian denominations.

1. Catholicism

In Catholic theology, pastoral ministry for the sick and infirm is one of the most significant ways that members of the Body of Christ continue the ministry and mission of Jesus. Pastoral ministry is considered to be the responsibility of all the baptized. Understood in the broad sense of "helping others", pastoral ministry is the responsibility of all Christians. Sacramental pastoral ministry is the administration of the sacraments (Baptism, Confirmation, Eucharist, Penance, Extreme Unction, Holy Orders, Matrimony) that is reserved to consecrated priests except for Baptism (in an emergency, anyone can baptize) and marriage, where the spouses are the ministers and the priest is the witness. Pastoral ministry was understood differently at different times in history. A significant development occurred after the Fourth Lateran Council in 1215 (more on this in the link to Father Boyle's lecture below). The Second Vatican Council (Vatican II) applied the word "pastoral" to a variety of situations involving care of souls; on this point, go to the link to Monsignor Gherardini's lecture).

Many Catholic parishes employ lay ecclesial ministers as "pastoral associates" or "pastoral assistants", lay people who serve in ministerial or administrative roles, assisting the priest in his work, but who are not ordained clerics. They are responsible, among other things, for the spiritual care of frail and housebound as well as for running a multitude of tasks associated with the sacramental life of the Church. If priests have the necessary qualifications in counseling or in psychotherapy, they may offer professional psychological services when they give pastoral counseling as part of their pastoral ministry of souls. However, the church hierarchy under John Paul II and Benedict XVI has emphasized that the Sacrament of Penance, or Reconciliation, is for the forgiveness of sins and not counseling and as such should not be confused with or incorporated into the therapy given to a person by a priest, even if the therapist priest is also their confessor. The two processes, both of which are privileged and confidential under civil and canon law, are separate by nature.

Youth workers and youth ministers are also finding a place within parishes (citation needed), and this involves their spirituality. It is common for Youth workers/ministers to be involved in pastoral ministry and are required to have a qualification in counseling before entering into this arm of ministry.

2.Orthodoxy

The priesthood obligations of Orthodox clergymen are outlined by John Chrysostom (347–407) in his treatise On the Priesthood. It is perhaps the first pastoral work written, although he was only a deacon when he penned it. It stresses the dignity of the priesthood. The priest, it says, is greater than kings, angels, or parents, but priests are for that reason most tempted to pride and ambition. They, more than anyone else, need clear and unshakable wisdom, patience that disarms pride, and exceptional prudence in dealing with souls.

3.Protestantism

This section is written like a personal reflection, personal essay, or argumentative essay that states a Wikipedia editor's personal feelings or presents an original argument about a topic. Please help improve it by rewriting it in an encyclopedic style. (June 2022) (Learn how and when to remove this template message)

There are many assumptions about what a pastor's ministry is. The core practices of a pastor's ministry in mainline Protestant churches include leading worship, preaching, pastoral care, outreach, and supporting the work of the congregation. Theological Seminaries provide a curriculum that supports these key facets of ministry. Pastors are often expected to also be involved in local ministries, such as hospital chaplaincy, visitation, funerals, weddings and organizing religious activities. "Pastoral ministry" includes outreach, encouragement, support, counseling and other care for members and friends of the congregation. In many churches, there are groups like deacons that provide outreach and support, often led and supported by the pastor.

For example, the Evangelical Wesleyan Church instructs clergy with the following words: "We should endeavor to assist those under our ministry, and to aid in the salvation of souls by instructing them in their homes. Family religion is waning in many branches. And what avails public preaching alone, though we could preach like angels? We must, yea, every traveling preacher must instruct the people from house to house." The Presbyterian Church (USA) is structured so that there is parity between lay leaders and pastors. Deacons and elders are ordained, with specific duties.

1.6. Clinical Pastoral Education

Clinical Pastoral Education (CPE) is education to teach spiritual care to clergy and others. CPE is the primary method of training hospital and hospice chaplains and spiritual care providers in the United States, Canada, Australia and New Zealand. CPE is both a multicultural and interfaith experience that uses real-life ministry encounters of students to improve the care provided by caregivers.

An underpinning theory of education that structures clinical pastoral education is the "Action-Reflection" mode of learning. CPE students typically compose "verbatim" of their pastoral care encounters in which they are invited to reflect upon what occurred and draw insight from these reflections that can be implemented in future pastoral care events.

1.History OF Clinical Pastoral Education

Although the practice of spiritual care has a long tradition in Christianity and to some extent in other faith traditions, the systematic analysis of practice associated with clinical pastoral education had its beginnings in the early 20th century. In 1925, Richard Cabot, a physician and adjunct lecturer at the Harvard Divinity School, published an article in Survey Graphic suggesting that every candidate for ministry receive clinical training for pastoral work similar to the clinical training offered to medical students. In the 1930s, the Reverend Anton Boisen placed theological students at the Chicago Theological Seminary in supervised contact with patients in mental hospitals, a flagship program that later resulted in the forming of the ACPE. In 1952, combining the work of Professor Paul E. Johnson and the philanthropy of Albert V. Danielsen, Boston University established within its School of Theology the Danielsen Pastoral Counseling Center, which was accredited by the American Association of Pastoral Counselors. Now the Danielsen Institute, it trains in its mental-health clinic doctoral candidates and fellows in pastoral counseling.

2.Accrediting bodies

CPE in Australia and New Zealand is conducted by six CPE accrediting associations that consult together for common curricula and standards of practice under an umbrella association, the Australia New Zealand Association of Clinical Pastoral Education (ANZACPE).[7] The six constituent associations are: New South Wales College of Clinical Pastoral Education (New South Wales and the Australian Capital Territory); Queensland Institute of Clinical Pastoral Education; Association for Supervised Pastoral Education in Australia (Victoria and Tasmania); Association for Clinical Pastoral Education in Western Australia; South Australia and Northern Territory Association for Clinical Pastoral Education; and New Zealand Association for Clinical Pastoral Education.

In the United States there are currently two organizations who are recognized by the United States Department of Education. The Association for Clinical Pastoral Education is recognized as an accrediting agency for CPE programs by the U.S. Department of Education. The Institute for Clinical Pastoral Training is accredited by the Accrediting Council for Continuing Education & Training (ACCET). ACCET is listed by the U.S. Department of Education as a nationally recognized accrediting agency. Likewise, there are over two hundred and seventy accredited seminary graduate programs with the Association of Theological Schools in the United States and Canada (ATS) in which some provide specializations in clinical pastoral education.

In Canada, all CPE training and accreditation is done through CASC/ACSS, the Canadian Association of Spiritual Care.

3.Faith Healing

Faith healing is the practice of prayer and gestures (such as laying on of hands) that are believed by some to elicit divine intervention in spiritual and physical healing, especially the Christian practice. Believers assert that the healing of disease and disability can be brought about by religious faith through prayer or other rituals that, according to adherents, can stimulate a divine presence and power. Religious belief in divine intervention does not depend on empirical evidence of an evidence-based outcome achieved via faith healing. Virtually all[a] scientists and philosophers dismiss faith healing as pseudoscience.

Claims that "a myriad of techniques" such as prayer, divine intervention, or the ministrations of an individual healer can cure illness have been popular throughout history. There have been claims that faith can cure blindness, deafness, cancer, HIV/AIDS, developmental disorders, anemia, arthritis, corns, defective speech, multiple sclerosis, skin rashes, total body paralysis, and various injuries. Recoveries have been attributed to many techniques commonly classified as faith healing. It can involve prayer, a visit to a religious shrine, or simply a strong belief in a supreme being.

Many people interpret the Bible, especially the New Testament, as teaching belief in, and the practice of, faith healing. According to a 2004 Newsweek poll, 72 percent of Americans said they believe that praying to God can cure someone, even if science says the person has an incurable disease. Unlike faith healing, advocates of spiritual healing make no attempt to seek divine intervention, instead believing in divine energy. The increased interest in alternative medicine at the end of the 20th century has given rise to a parallel interest among sociologists in the relationship of religion to health.

Faith healing can be classified as a spiritual, supernatural, or paranormal topic, and, in some cases, belief in faith healing can be classified as magical thinking. The American Cancer Society states "available scientific evidence does not support claims that faith healing can actually cure physical ailments". "Death, disability, and other unwanted outcomes have occurred when faith healing was elected instead of medical care for serious injuries or illnesses. "When parents have practiced faith healing rather than medical care, many children have died that otherwise would have been expected to live. Similar results are found in adults.

Regarded as a Christian belief that God heals people through the power of the Holy Spirit, faith healing often involves the laying on of hands. It is also called supernatural healing, divine healing, and miracle healing, among other things. Healing in the Bible is often associated with the ministry of specific individuals including Elijah, Jesus and Paul.

Christian physician Reginald B. Cherry views faith healing as a pathway of healing in which God uses both the natural and the supernatural to heal. Being healed has been described as a privilege of accepting Christ's redemption on the cross. Pentecostal writer Wilfred Graves Jr. views the healing of the body as a physical expression of salvation. Matthew 8:17, after describing Jesus exorcising at sunset and healing all of the sick who were brought to him, quotes these miracles as a fulfillment of the prophecy in Isaiah 53:5: "He took up our infirmities and carried our diseases".

Even those Christian writers who believe in faith healing do not all believe that one's faith presently brings about the desired healing. "your faith does not affect your healing now. When you are healed rests entirely on what the sovereign purposes of the Healer are(Larry,2001) cautions against allowing enthusiasm for faith healing to stir up false hopes. "Just believing hard enough, long enough or strong enough will not strengthen you or prompt your healing. Doing mental gymnastics to 'hold on to your miracle' will not cause your healing to manifest now." Those who actively lay hands on others and pray with them to be healed are usually aware that healing may not always follow immediately. Proponents of faith healing say it may come later, and it may not come in this life. "The truth is that your healing may manifest in eternity, not in time".

1.7. New Testament

This section uncritically uses texts from within a religion or faith system without referring to secondary sources that critically analyze them. Please help improve this article by adding references to reliable secondary sources, with multiple points of view. (September 2015) (Learn how and when to remove this template message). Parts of the four canonical gospels in the New Testament say that Jesus cured physical ailments well outside the capacity of first-century medicine. Jesus' healing acts are considered miraculous and spectacular due to the results being impossible or statistically improbable. One example is the case of "a woman who had had a discharge of blood for twelve years, and who had suffered much under many physicians, and had spent all that she had, and was not better but rather grew worse". After healing her, Jesus tells her "Daughter, your faith has made you well. Go in peace! Be cured from your illness". At least two other times Jesus credited the sufferer's faith as the means of being healed: Mark 10:52 and Luke 19:10.

Jesus endorsed the use of the medical assistance of the time (medicines of oil and wine) when he told the parable of the Good Samaritan (Luke 10:25–37), who "bound up [an injured man's] wounds, pouring on oil and wine" (verse 34) as a physician would. Jesus then told the doubting teacher of the law (who had elicited this parable by his self-justifying question, "And who is my neighbor?" in verse 29) to "go, and do likewise" in loving others with whom he would never ordinarily associate (verse 37).

The healing in the gospels is referred to as a "sign" to prove Jesus' divinity and to foster belief in him as the Christ. However, when asked for other types of miracles, Jesus refused some but granted others in consideration of the motive of the request. Some theologians' understanding is that Jesus healed all who were present every single time. Sometimes he determines whether they had faith that he would heal them. Four of the seven miraculous signs performed in the Fourth Gospel that indicated he was sent from God were acts of healing or resurrection. He heals the Capernaum official's son, heals a paralytic by the pool in Bethsaida, healing a man born blind, and resurrecting Lazarus of Bethany.

Jesus told his followers to heal the sick and stated that signs such as healing are evidence of faith. Jesus also told his followers to "cure sick people, raise up dead persons, make lepers clean, expel demons. You received free, give free".

Jesus sternly ordered many who received healing from him: "Do not tell anyone!" Jesus did not approve of anyone asking for a sign just for the spectacle of it, describing such as coming from a "wicked and adulterous generation".

The apostle Paul believed healing is one of the special gifts of the Holy Spirit, and that the possibility exists that certain persons may possess this gift to an extraordinarily high degree.

In the New Testament Epistle of James, the faithful are told that to be healed, those who are sick should call upon the elders of the church to pray over [them] and anoint [them] with oil in the name of the Lord.

The New Testament says that during Jesus' ministry and after his Resurrection, the apostles healed the sick and cast out demons, made lame men walk, raised the dead and performed other miracles. Apostles were holy men who had direct access to God and could channel his power to help and heal people. For example, Saint Peter healed a disabled man.

Jesus used miracles to convince people that he was inaugurating the Messianic Age, as in Mt 12.28. Scholars have described Jesus' miracles as establishing the kingdom during his lifetime.

ACTIVITY 1.2: CASE STUDY

Blessing Baptist church Mogadishu recruited a counselor to children. The children complaint that the counselor hardly attends to their situations.

In a group, discuss why some counselors do not care about their fellow clients?

1.8. Early Christian Church

Accounts or references to healing appear in the writings of many Ante Nicene Fathers, although many of these mentions are very general and do not include specifics.

1. Catholicism

The Roman Catholic Church recognizes two "not mutually exclusive" kinds of healing, one justified by science and one justified by faith:

healing by human "natural means, through the practice of medicine" which emphasizes that the theological virtue of "charity demands that we not neglect natural means of healing people who are ill" and the cardinal virtue of prudence forewarns not "to employ a technique that has no scientific support (or even plausibility)"

healing by divine grace "interceded on behalf of the sick through the invocation of the name of the Lord Jesus, asking for healing through the power of the Holy Spirit, whether in the form of the sacramental laying on of hands and anointing with oil or of simple prayers for healing, which often include an appeal to the saints for their aid"

In 2000, the Congregation for the Doctrine of the Faith issued "Instruction on prayers for healing" with specific norms about prayer meetings for obtaining healing, which presents the Catholic Church's doctrines of sickness and healing.

It accepts "that there may be means of natural healing that have not yet been understood or recognized by science", but it rejects superstitious practices which are neither compatible with Christian teaching nor compatible with scientific evidence.

Faith healing is reported by Catholics as the result of intercessory prayer to a saint or to a person with the gift of healing. According to U.S. Catholic magazine, "Even in this skeptical, postmodern, scientific age miracles really are possible." According to a Newsweek poll, three-fourths of American Catholics say they pray for "miracles" of some sort.

According to John Cavadini(2001), when healing is granted, "The miracle is not primarily for the person healed, but for all people, as a sign of God's work in the ultimate healing called 'salvation', or a sign of the kingdom that is coming." Some might view their own healing as a sign they are particularly worthy or holy, while others do not deserve it.

The Catholic Church has a special Congregation dedicated to the careful investigation of the validity of alleged miracles attributed to prospective saints. Pope Francis tightened the rules on money and miracles in the canonization process. Since Catholic Christians believe the lives of canonized saints in the Church will reflect Christ's, many have come to expect healing miracles. While the popular conception of a miracle can be wide-ranging, the Catholic Church has a specific definition for the kind of miracle formally recognized in a canonization process.

According to Catholic Encyclopedia, it is often said that cures at shrines and during Christian pilgrimages are mainly due to psychotherapy – partly to confident trust in Divine providence, and partly to the strong expectancy of cure that comes over suggestible persons at these times and places.

Among the best-known accounts by Catholics of faith healings are those attributed to the miraculous intercession of the apparition of the Blessed Virgin Mary known as Our Lady of Lourdes at the Sanctuary of Our Lady of Lourdes in France and the remissions of life-threatening disease claimed by those who have applied for aid to Saint Jude, who is known as the "patron saint of lost causes".

As of 2004, Catholic medics have asserted that there have been 67 miracles and 7,000 unexplainable medical cures at Lourdes since 1855. In a 1908 book, it says these cures were subjected to intense medical scrutiny and were only recognized as authentic spiritual cures after a commission of doctors and scientists, called the Lourdes Medical Bureau, had ruled out any physical mechanism for the patient's recovery.

2.Evangelicalism

Laying on of hands for healing in Living Streams International Church, Accra, Ghana, 2018. In some Pentecostal and Charismatic Evangelical churches, a special place is thus reserved for faith healings with laying on of hands during worship services or for campaigns evangelization. Faith healing or divine healing is considered to be an inheritance of Jesus acquired by his death and resurrection. Biblical inerrancy ensures that the miracles and healings described in the Bible are still relevant and may be present in the life of the believer.

At the beginning of the 20th century, the new Pentecostal movement drew participants from the Holiness movement and other movements in America that already believed in divine healing. By the 1930s, several faith healers drew large crowds and established worldwide followings.

The first Pentecostals in the modern sense appeared in Topeka, Kansas, in a Bible school conducted by Charles Fox Parham, a holiness teacher and former Methodist pastor. Pentecostalism achieved worldwide attention in 1906 through the Azusa Street Revival in Los Angeles led by William Joseph Seymour.

Smith Wigglesworth was also a well-known figure in the early part of the 20th century. A former English plumber turned evangelist who lived simply and read nothing but the Bible from the time his wife taught him to read, Wigglesworth traveled around the world preaching about Jesus and performing faith healings. Wigglesworth claimed to raise several people from the dead in Jesus' name in his meetings.

During the 1920s and 1930s, Aimee Simple McPherson was a controversial faith healer of growing popularity during the Great Depression. Subsequently, William M. Branham has been credited as the initiator of the post-World War II healing revivals. The healing revival he began led many to emulate his style and spawned a generation of faith healers. Because of this, Branham has been recognized as the "father of modern faith healers". According to writer and researcher Patsy Sims, "the power of a Branham service and his stage presence remains a legend unparalleled in the history of the Charismatic movement". By the late 1940s, Oral Roberts, who was associated with and promoted by Branham's Voice of Healing magazine also became well known, and he continued with faith healing until the 1980s. Roberts discounted faith healing in the late 1950s, stating, "I never was a faith healer and I was never raised that way. My parents believed very strongly in medical science and we have a doctor who takes care of our children when they get sick. I cannot heal anyone – God does that." A friend of Roberts was Kathryn Kuhlman, another popular faith healer, who gained fame in the 1950s and had a television program on CBS. Also in this era, Jack Coe and A. A. Allen were faith healers who traveled with large tents for large open-air crusades.

Oral Roberts's successful use of television as a medium to gain a wider audience led others to follow suit. His former pilot, Kenneth Copeland, started a healing ministry. Pat Robertson, Benny Hinn, and Kenneth kopler became well-known televangelists who claimed to heal the sick. Richard Rossi is known for advertising his healing clinics through secular television and radio. Kuhlman influenced Benny Hinn, who adopted some of her techniques and wrote a book about her.

3.Christian Science

Christian Science claims that healing is possible through prayer based on an understanding of God and the underlying spiritual perfection of God's creation. The material world as humanly perceived is believed to not be the spiritual reality. Christian Scientists believe that healing through prayer is possible insofar as it succeeds in bringing the spiritual reality of health into human experience. Christian Scientists believe that prayer does not change the spiritual creation but gives a clearer view of it, and the result appears in the human scene as healing: the human picture adjusts to coincide more nearly with the divine reality. Christian Scientists do not consider themselves to be faith healers since faith or belief in Christian Science is not required on the part of the patient, and because they consider it reliable and provable rather than random.

Although there is no hierarchy in Christian Science, Christian Science practitioners devote full time to prayer for others on a professional basis, and advertise in an online directory published by the church. Christian Scientists sometimes tell their stories of healing at weekly testimony meetings at local Christian Science churches, or publish them in the church's magazines including The Christian Science Journal printed monthly since 1883, the Christian Science Sentinel printed weekly since 1898, and The Herald of Christian Science a foreign language magazine beginning with a German edition in 1903 and later expanding to Spanish, French, and Portuguese editions. Christian Science Reading Rooms often have archives of such healing accounts.

3.The Church of Jesus Christ of Latter-day Saints

The Church of Jesus Christ of Latter-day Saints (LDS) has had a long history of faith healings. Many members of the LDS Church have told their stories of healing within the LDS publication, the Ensign. The church believes healings come most often as a result of priesthood blessings given by the laying on of hands; however, prayer often accompanied with fasting is also thought to cause healings. Healing is always attributed to be God's power. Latter-day Saints believe that the Priesthood of God, held by prophets (such as Moses) and worthy disciples of the Savior, was restored via heavenly messengers to the first prophet of this dispensation, Joseph Smith.

According to LDS doctrine, even though members may have the restored priesthood authority to heal in the name of Jesus Christ, all efforts should be made to seek the appropriate medical help. Brigham Young stated this effectively, while also noting that the ultimate outcome is still dependent on the will of God.

If we are sick, and ask the Lord to heal us, and to do all for us that is necessary to be done, according to my understanding of the Gospel of salvation, I might as well ask the Lord to cause my wheat and corn to grow, without my plowing the ground and casting in the seed. It appears consistent to me to apply every remedy that comes within the range of my knowledge, and to ask my Father in Heaven, in the name of Jesus Christ, to sanctify that application to the healing of my body.

But suppose we were traveling in the mountains, and one or two were taken sick, without anything in the world in the shape of healing medicine within our reach, what should we do? According to my faith, ask the Lord Almighty to heal the sick. This is our privilege, when so situated that we cannot get anything to help ourselves. Then the Lord and his servants can do all. But it is my duty to do, when I have it in my power.

We lay hands on the sick and wish them to be healed, and pray the Lord to heal them, but we cannot always say that he will.

5.Islam

A number of healing traditions exist among Muslims. Some healers are particularly focused on diagnosing cases of possession by jinn or demons.

6.Buddhism

Chinese-born Australian businessman Jun Hong Lu was a prominent proponent of the "Guan Yin Citta Dharma Door", claiming that practicing the three "golden practices" of reciting texts and mantras, liberation of beings, and making vows, laid a solid foundation for improved physical, mental, and psychological well-being, with many followers publicly attesting to have been healed through practice.

7. Scientology

Some critics of Scientology have referred to some of its practices as being similar to faith healing, based on claims made by L. Ron Hubbard in Dianetics: The Modern Science of Mental Health and other writings.

8. Scientific investigation

Nearly all[a] scientists dismiss faith healing as pseudoscience. Believers assert that faith healing makes no scientific claims and thus should be treated as a matter of faith that is not testable by science. Critics reply that claims of medical cures should be tested scientifically because, although faith in the supernatural is not in itself usually considered to be the purview of science, claims of reproducible effects are nevertheless subject to scientific investigation.

Scientists and doctors generally find that faith healing lacks biological plausibility or epistemic warrant, which is one of the criteria used to judge whether clinical research is ethical and financially justified. A Cochrane review of intercessory prayer found "although some of the results of individual studies suggest a positive effect of intercessory prayer, the majority do not". The authors concluded: "We are not convinced that further trials of this intervention should be undertaken and would prefer to see any resources available for such a trial used to investigate other questions in health care".

A review in 1954 investigated spiritual healing, therapeutic touch and faith healing. Of the hundred cases reviewed, none revealed that the healer's intervention alone resulted in any improvement or cure of a measurable organic disability.

In addition, at least one study has suggested that adult Christian Scientists, who generally use prayer rather than medical care, have a higher death rate than other people of the same age.

The Global Medical Research Institute (GMRI) was created in 2012 to start collecting medical records of patients who claim to have received a supernatural healing miracle as a result of Christian Spiritual Healing practices. The organization has a panel of medical doctors who review the patient's records looking at entries prior to the claimed miracles and entries after the miracle was claimed to have taken place. "The overall goal of GMRI is to promote an empirically grounded understanding of the physiological, emotional, and sociological effects of Christian Spiritual Healing practices". This is accomplished by applying the same rigorous standards used in other forms of medical and scientific research.

A 2011 article in the New Scientist magazine cited positive physical results from meditation, positive thinking and spiritual faith.

9.Criticism

John Dominic says ''I have visited Lourdes in France and Fatima in Portugal, healing shrines of the Christian Virgin Mary. I have also visited Epidaurus in Greece and Pergamum in Turkey, healing shrines of the pagan god Asklepios. The miraculous healings recorded in both places were remarkably the same''. There are, for example, many crutches hanging in the grotto of Lourdes, mute witness to those who arrived lame and left whole. There are, however, no prosthetic limbs among them, no witnesses to paraplegics whose lost limbs were restored.

Skeptics of faith healing offer primarily two explanations for anecdotes of cures or improvements, relieving any need to appeal to the supernatural. The first is post hoc ergo propter hoc, meaning that a genuine improvement or spontaneous remission may have been experienced coincidental with but independent from anything the faith healer or patient did or said. These patients would have improved just as well even had they done nothing. The second is the placebo effect, through which a person may experience genuine pain relief and other symptomatic alleviation. In this case, the patient genuinely has been helped by the faith healer or faith-based remedy, not through any mysterious or numinous function, but by the power of their own belief that they would be healed. In both cases the patient may experience a real reduction in symptoms, though in neither case has anything miraculous or inexplicable occurred. Both cases, however, are strictly limited to the body's natural abilities.

According to the American Cancer Society available scientific evidence does not support claims that faith healing can actually cure physical ailments... One review published in 1998 looked at 172 cases of deaths among children treated by faith healing instead of conventional methods. These researchers estimated that if conventional treatment had been given, the survival rate for most of these children would have been more than 90 percent, with the remainder of the children also having a good chance of survival. A more recent study found that more than 200 children had died of treatable illnesses in the United States over the past thirty years because their parents relied on spiritual healing rather than conventional medical treatment.

The American Medical Association considers that prayer as therapy should not be a medically reimbursable or deductible expense.

Belgian philosopher and skeptic Etienne Vermeersch coined the term Lourdes effect as a criticism of the magical thinking and placebo effect possibilities for the claimed miraculous cures as there are no documented events where a severed arm has been reattached through faith healing at Lourdes. Vermeersch identifies ambiguity and equivocal nature of the miraculous cures as a key feature of miraculous events.

1.9. Negative impact on public health

Reliance on faith healing to the exclusion of other forms of treatment can have a public health impact when it reduces or eliminates access to modern medical techniques. This is evident in both higher mortality rates for children and in reduced life expectancy for adults. Critics have also made note of serious injury that has resulted from falsely labelled "healings", where patients erroneously consider themselves cured and cease or withdraw from treatment. For example, at least six people have died after faith healing by their church and being told they had been healed of HIV and could stop taking their medications. It is the stated position of the AMA that "prayer as therapy should not delay access to traditional medical care". Choosing faith healing while rejecting modern medicine can and does cause people to die needlessly.

1.Christian theological criticism of faith healing

Christian theological criticism of faith healing broadly falls into two distinct levels of disagreement.

The first is widely termed the "open-but-cautious" view of the miraculous in the church today. This term is deliberately used by Robert L. Saucy in the book Are Miraculous Gifts for Today? Don Carson is another example of a Christian teacher who has put forward what has been described as an "open-but-cautious" view. In dealing with the claims of Warfield, particularly "Warfield's insistence that miracles ceased" Carson asserts, "But this argument stands up only if such miraculous gifts are theologically tied exclusively to a role of attestation; and that is demonstrably not so." However, while affirming that he does not expect healing to happen today, Carson is critical of aspects of the faith healing movement, "Another issue is that of immense abuses in healing practices. The most common form of abuse is the view that since all illness is directly or indirectly attributable to the devil and his works, and since Christ by his cross has defeated the devil, and by his Spirit has given us the power to overcome him, healing is the inheritance right of all true Christians who call upon the Lord with genuine faith."

The second level of theological disagreement with Christian faith healing goes further. Commonly referred to as cessationism, its adherents either claim that faith healing will not happen today at all, or may happen today, but it would be unusual. Richard Gaffin argues for a form of cessationism in an essay alongside Saucy's in the book Are Miraculous Gifts for Today? In his book Perspectives on Pentecost Gaffin states of healing and related gifts that "the conclusion to be drawn is that as listed in 1 Corinthians 12 and encountered throughout the narrative in Acts, these gifts, particularly when exercised regularly by a given individual, are part of the foundational structure of the church and so have passed out of the life of the church." Gaffin qualifies this, however, by saying "At the same time, however, the sovereign will and power of God today to heal the sick, particularly in response to prayer (see e.g. James 5:14, 15), ought to be acknowledged and insisted on."

2. Fraud

Skeptics of faith healers point to fraudulent practices either in the healings themselves (such as plants in the audience with fake illnesses), or concurrent with the healing work supposedly taking place and claim that faith healing is a quack practice in which the "healers" use well known non-supernatural illusions to exploit credulous people in order to obtain their gratitude, confidence and money. James Randi's The Faith Healers investigates Christian evangelists such as Peter Popoff, who claimed to heal sick people on stage in front of an audience. Popoff pretended to know private details about participants' lives by receiving radio transmissions from his wife who was off-stage and had gathered information from audience members prior to the show. According to this book, many of the leading modern evangelistic healers have engaged in deception and fraud. The book also questioned how faith healers use funds that were sent to them for specific purposes. [k] Physicist Robert L. Park and doctor and consumer advocate Stephen Barrett[7] have called into question the ethics of some exorbitant fees.

There have also been legal controversies. For example, in 1955 at a Jack Coe revival service in Miami, Florida, Coe told the parents of a three-year-old boy that he healed their son who had polio. Coe then told the parents to remove the boy's leg braces. However, their son was not cured of polio and removing the braces left the boy in constant pain. As a result, through the efforts of Joseph L. Lewis, Coe was arrested and charged on February 6, 1956, with practicing medicine without a license, a felony in the state of Florida. A Florida Justice of the Peace dismissed the case on grounds that Florida exempts divine healing from the law. Later that year Coe was diagnosed with bulbar polio, and died a few weeks later at Dallas' Parkland Hospital on December 17, 1956.

3.Miracles for sale

TV personality Derren Brown produced a show on faith healing entitled Miracles for Sale which arguably exposed the art of faith healing as a scam. In this show, Derren trained a scuba diver trainer picked from the general public to be a faith healer and took him to Texas to successfully deliver a faith healing session to a congregation.

4. United States law

The 1974 Child Abuse Prevention and Treatment Act (CAPTA) required states to grant religious exemptions to child neglect and child abuse laws in order to receive federal money. The CAPTA amendments of 1996 42 U.S.C. § 5106i state:

(a) In General. – Nothing in this Act shall be construed –

"(1) as establishing a Federal requirement that a parent or legal guardian provide a child any medical service or treatment against the religious beliefs of the parent or legal guardian; and "(2) to require that a State find, or to prohibit a State from finding, abuse or neglect in cases in which a parent or legal guardian relies solely or partially upon spiritual means rather than medical treatment, in accordance with the religious beliefs of the parent or legal guardian.

"(b) State Requirement. – Notwithstanding subsection (a), a State shall, at a minimum, have in place authority under State law to permit the child protective services system of the State to pursue any legal remedies, including the authority to initiate legal proceedings in a court of competent jurisdiction, to provide medical care or treatment for a child when such care or treatment is necessary to prevent or remedy serious harm to the child, or to prevent the withholding of medically indicated treatment from children with life threatening conditions. Except with respect to the withholding of medically indicated treatments from disabled infants with life threatening conditions, case by case determinations concerning the exercise of the authority of this subsection shall be within the sole discretion of the State.

Thirty-one states have child-abuse religious exemptions. These are Alabama, Alaska, California, Colorado, Delaware, Florida, Georgia, Idaho, Illinois,

Indiana, Iowa, Kansas, Kentucky, Louisiana, Maine, Michigan, Minnesota, Mississippi, Missouri, Montana, Nevada, New Hampshire, New Jersey, New Mexico, Ohio, Oklahoma, Oregon, Pennsylvania, Vermont, Virginia, and Wyoming. In six of these states, Arkansas, Idaho, Iowa, Louisiana, Ohio and Virginia, the exemptions extend to murder and manslaughter. Of these, Idaho is the only state accused of having a large number of deaths due to the legislation in recent times. In February 2015, controversy was sparked in Idaho over a bill believed to further reinforce parental rights to deny their children medical care.

5. Reckless homicide convictions

Parents have been convicted of child abuse and felony reckless negligent homicide and found responsible for killing their children when they withheld lifesaving medical care and chose only prayers.

ACTIVITY 1.3

1. Evaluate the criticism of pastoral care from different religious organizations-

----

Conclusions

Pastoral care personnel must be careful with what they do. The job requires someone with well-informed backgrounds and skills since the job of care and counseling is very delicate to perform. Pastoral healers must adhere to biblical models of healing and therapy within and outside the faith community.

Chapter References

1."University of Canberra, Multi-faith Centre". Archived from the original on 2013-06-21. Pastoral care is an ancient model of emotional and spiritual support that can be found in all cultures and traditions. Historically Christian but is now a multi faith community.

2. Hélène Mulholland (25 October 2017). "Jane Flint: 'Having an atheist chaplain is about patient choice'". The Guardian. Retrieved 5 February 2018.

3.NHS Chaplaincy Guidelines 2015" (PDF). NHS England. Retrieved 18 January 2019. Act new guidance is provided for the care of patients and service users whatever their religion or belief.

4.Savage, David (2018). "3: Public perceptions of chaplains and non-religious pastoral care. Religious and non-religious beliefs in society". Non-Religious Pastoral Care: A Practical Guide. Routledge. pp. 34–56. ISBN 9781351264464. Retrieved 18 January 2019. "NSW Government, Department of Education". 26 July 2021. "University of Canberra, Multi-faith Centre". Archived from the original on 2013-06-21.

6. Rizzuto, Ana-María (March 1998). "Psychoanalytic Psychotherapy and Pastoral Guidance". Journal of Pastoral Care. 52 (1): 69–78. 7.doi:10.1177/002234099805200109. ISSN 0022-3409.

8. Woldemichael, Meaza T.; Broesterhuizen, Marcel; Liègeois, Axel (December 2013). "Christian Pastoral Care and Psychotherapy: A Need for Theoretical Clarity". Journal of Pastoral Care & Counseling: Advancing theory and professional practice through scholarly and reflective publications. 67 (4): 1–13. doi:10.1177/154230501306700406. ISSN 1542-3050.

9.Cole, Allan Hugh (2010-07-09). "What Makes Care Pastoral?". Pastoral Psychology. 59 (6): 711–723. doi:10.1007/s11089-010-0296-5. ISSN 0031-2789.

"University of Canberra, Multi-faith Centre". Archived from the original on 2013-06-21. "Ephesians 4:10–12". Retrieved 2008-12-09.

10.Rowdon, Harold (2002). Church Leaders Hand Book. p. 227. ISBN 978-0-900128-23-3.

11.Lexikon fur Theologie und Kirche (in German).

12.Morgenthaler, Christoph (2012-04-04), "Verzeichnis der Veröffentlichungen", Nachdenkliche Seelsorge - seelsorgliches Nachdenken, Göttingen: Vandenhoeck & Ruprecht, pp. 342–351, retrieved 2023-08-20

13."Philip Schaff: NPNF2-08. Basil: Letters and Select Works - Christian Classics Ethereal Library". www.ccel.org. Retrieved 2023-08-20. "pastoral psychology". www.pastoralpsychologie.de. Retrieved 2023-08-18. "Humanist Pastoral Support". Humanists UK. Retrieved 5 February 2018.

14.The Discipline of the Evangelical Wesleyan Church. Evangelical Wesleyan Church. 2015. p. 108. (U.S.A.), Presbyterian Church (1994). The Constitution of the Presbyterian.

15.Cobb, Puchalski and Rumbold (eds.), Oxford Textbook of Spirituality in Healthcare, 2012, p. 417. "Frequently Asked Questions about ACPE Clinical

Pastoral Education". The Association for Clinical Pastoral Education, Inc. See section What is Clinical Pastoral Education. Archived from the original on 2011-10-12. Retrieved 2011-10-20.

16. Cobb, Puchalski and Rumbold (eds.), Oxford Textbook of Spirituality in Healthcare, 2012, p. 294.

17. Stokoe, Rodney J.R. (2005) [1974], "Clinical Pastoral Education" (PDF), The Nova Scotia Medical Bulletin (Reprint), 53 (1): 26–28, ISSN 0029-5094, archived from the original (PDF) on 2011-09-29, retrieved 2011-10-20 The reprint is available as part of the project: "Living Human Memories". CASC/ACSS The Canadian Association for Spiritual Care. Archived from the original on 2011-06-22. Retrieved 2011-10-20.

18. "American Association of Pastoral Counselors/History". Archived from the original on 2009-04-03. Retrieved 2019-05-07.

19. "History of the Danielsen Institute". Archived from the original on 2009-09-08.

20. "Aspea - Anzacpe". Archived from the original on 2014-01-25. Retrieved 2014-03-07.

21. "Specialized Accrediting Agencies". U.S. Department of Education. Retrieved 2013-07-04.

22. "The Institute for Clinical Pastoral Training". "U.S. Department of Education". 27 October 2022.

23. "The Association of Theological Schools". www.ats.edu. Retrieved 2022-09-

CHAPTER TWO

Pastoral Care Profession

2.1. Introduction

A person who is engaged in the care and support of the inner person is known as a Pastoral care worker. Formal religious denominations do not necessarily govern this role as they generally provide support for the individual's belief systems, regardless of denomination or affiliation.

2.2. What does a Pastoral Care Worker Do?

A Pastoral Care Worker is a trained, experienced and compassionate person who joins a business, school, or organization to provide additional spiritual support to clients, their families and staff. Pastoral Care Worker services provided are often non-denominational, although they may represent a particular church.

Pastoral Care Workers are positive role models who bring genuine compassion, understanding and practical ongoing support to their clients. They achieve this by providing a safe space for the client to talk about their experiences, share concerns, and just provide spiritual and emotional support as required.

Pastoral Care Workers work alongside and complement other welfare staff, such as social workers and counsellors, to advance the well-being of clients and employees.

2.3. Common Tasks and Duties of a Pastoral Care Worker:

The main duties of a Pastoral Care Worker are:

1. Support the physical, emotional, mental and spiritual well-being of clients, staff, and families through times of transition, stress, grief and loss.

2. Encourage spiritual growth

Support the organization in its aim to be a safe and supportive working environment

3. Link families to community support resources and services as required

4. Promote self-care and spiritual wellbeing within the organization

2.4. What skills do I need to become a Pastoral Care Worker?

The role of Pastoral Care Worker often attracts individuals who are deeply compassionate, interested in supporting others through difficult times, and have a high level of empathy.

Individuals with formal training in pastoral care are expected to have skills that enable them to discuss religious matters and provide support to all people with spiritual and emotional needs. Pastoral care workers may use empathy, listening, reminiscence, or simply being with clients to engage with them more deeply in order to assist them as required.

2.5. Additional skills that could be beneficial include:

1. Ability to build rapport easily and communicate with people from different backgrounds

2. Provide person-centered pastoral care

3. Working understanding of people's cultural background, denominations and faith traditions.

4. Ability to respond to people in need

5. Provide counselling or referral to services as required

6. Understanding to care for pastoral and spiritual concerns as requested

7. Effective written and verbal communication skills

8. The ability to deal with high-stress situations, e.g., with people with physical and mental health challenges, dealing with end-of-life situations, coping with trauma and violence.

2.6. What are the types of organizations a Pastoral Care Worker Works At?

Pastoral Care workers work as a part of a care team in a variety of settings, including:

Hospitals

Schools

Churches

Prisons

Aged care facilities

Community Outreach Organizations.

he main duties of a Pastoral Care Worker are: Support the physical, emotional, mental and spiritual well-being of clients, staff, and families through times of transition, stress, grief and loss. Encourage spiritual growth. Support them in some point in life, everyone travels a difficult journey or situation. Whether it be grief, depression, loss, sickness, loneliness or more, people sometimes travel this path alone, not having anyone they feel they can turn to.

Pastoral care can take many different forms in the church. It's far more than just "caregiving", it provides for many different people in various aspects of life both in and outside of the church. Continue reading to learn more about pastoral care and its role in today's world.

2.7. Explore: Pastoral Care Then and Now

Pastoral care dates back to the New Testament, where many indications state that the early church was caring for its members as individuals through the Christian community (Acts 5 and 6). Pastoral care has always held special importance in Christian communities. Many state that pastoral care in the early days of the church was shaped through biblical and theological perspectives, which carries through today.

One of the biggest differences between pastoral care then and now is that there is a much greater investment in the care given and received today, as pastoral care goes far beyond inside the church. Rather than praying for the sick or others in the church, pastoral care is given and received in hospitals, nursing homes, personal residences and anywhere that someone may reside that wishes for spiritual guidance, prayer or care.

Another difference is that pastoral care was only provided by men early on. For more than six decades in The United Methodist Church, women have had full clergy rights, allowing women and men the opportunity to serve in their ministry and Methodist teachings through pastoral care.

Activity 2.1

1. what does pastoral care givers do? --

----

2. what differentiate caregivers from counselors? ------------------------------

----

2.8. Why is Pastoral Care Needed Now More Than Ever?

Today's world faces family and relationship turmoil, injustices, increased isolation and loneliness, a lack of community and overall divide. Social media, the global pandemic, heightened political divisions and increased violence all could be considered parts of the suffering occurring in people's lives.

The increased polarization is affecting people every day, and our communities are hurting, with some feeling like they have no one to confide in. In fact, a study published in the American Sociological Review states that the average person in the U.S. only has one close friend, whereas one in four people report they have no confidantes at all.

Churches have witnessed a divide and a decrease in attendance, elder numbers and new church openings. However, pastoral care can help those who feel they have no one to turn to. Even if someone is hurting and is unable to attend worship; even if they haven't been to church in a while; even if they feel like they've neglected or gotten lost in their faith; pastoral care can help guide and heal suffering.

2.9. What is Expected of Pastoral Care Practices?

Pastoral care provides spiritual aid in many aspects. Pastoral care is an essential part of ministry for those to serve the local church and serve through Christ's love and justice and provides emotional, social and spiritual support for those in need or who are suffering a crisis alone. This care and support can also provide nurturing through prayer.

The *main **practices of pastoral** care* include:

1. Spiritual care. Simply put, spiritual care is attending to a person's spiritual or religious needs as they cope with pain, loss, loneliness or illness by helping them heal physically and emotionally and regain their sense of spiritual well-being.

2. Healing ministry. Those that are ordained or elders in the United Methodist Church may include healing prayer in their worship services. The healing ministry may take place at Holy Communion or may be offered weekly, monthly or quarterly, and those who can attend worship are invited to participate and slowly heal with others.

3. Assistance with trauma. Through times of pain and crisis, pastoral care can offer support, prayer, discussions, spiritual guidance and more to help create ongoing communication.

4. Praying with and for others. Prayer during times of sickness, hurting and healing can be extremely powerful and comforting. Pastoral care offers a safe space to pray with those in their own location and who may not be able to physically attend worship.

5. Biblical counseling. Using the Bible as a guide and a reference, pastoral care can aid in one's spiritual journey, whether they want to further it or they may have lost their way and are ready to continue their spiritual pathway.

Bereavement. Throughout life, we all experience loss and grief. Pastoral care can aid in bereavement services, such as meeting with someone one-on-one or holding weekly or monthly sessions, by assisting people who are rebuilding or continuing their life through prayer.

Each of these responsibilities and duties play an important role in pastoral care, as pastoral care can serve the needs of many different people, such as:

The sick and homebound

Those who feel lost or lonely

The forgotten and marginalized

Those who are grieving

People suffering mental health disorders, such as depression, anxiety or PTSD

Those who have been abused, mistreated or suffer from a traumatic event

Those who want to strengthen their faith.

A skilled pastoral care professional will also recognize when to refer someone to a trained mental health professional with more specialized skills.

2.10. Is Providing Pastoral Care the Right Fit for Your Skillset?

You may be wondering if you should take the needed steps to provide pastoral care in your church and your community. Take a step back and ask yourself these questions:

Do you possess Christian leadership skills that can help spiritually guide others?

Are you passionate about your faith and living out God's word?

Do you have the gifts needed to care for and assist others?

Do your God-given gifts mentally and emotionally affect and connect with others in a meaningful and positive way?

Do you want to help others find peace, hope and love through God's word and spiritual guidance?

If you answered yes to one or more of the questions above, you may consider continuing your personal ministry through pastoral care. Clergy members and leaders can participate in providing pastoral care. In fact, more than 1,700 United Methodist clergy have been endorsed to answer God's call by taking their ministry beyond the church.

Attend Theology School to Deepen Your Pastoral Care Training at Perkins

At Perkins School of Theology, we are a diverse community that welcomes all Christian voices. Throughout your time at Perkins, we will strive to help you discern, utilize and test your gifts, guiding you and equipping you with the skills needed to practice pastoral care, or whatever else God has called you to do.

We honor your unique worth, and offer many different pathways and graduate degrees to continue growing your vocational goals and invite you to explore them. organization in its aim to be a safe and supportive working environment.

Pastoral care has always been of special importance in the Christian community. The biographies of the great charismatic ministers, beginning with the Fathers of the Eastern church and the Western church, testify to surprising variations of this pastoral care. The principal interest of pastoral care whether exercised by clergy or laity is the personal welfare of persons who are hurt, troubled, alienated, or confused within. The historical expressions of pastoral care have focused on the predominant but not exclusive expressions of ultimate concern characteristic of the period in question. St. Ignatius, for example, addressed the terror of death when he termed the sacrament "the medicine of immortality." Luther responded to the conscience tortured by guilt and uncertainty by proclaiming the free forgiveness of sin by grace alone, apart from human accomplishment. The modern Christian community has utilized the insights of psychology and psychiatry in developing pastoral counseling and therapy responsive to modern anxieties. Fundamentally, however, pastoral care has always attempted to respond to the totality of human needs in every age in consonance with the words of Jesus Christ: "I was hungry and you gave me food, I was thirsty and you gave me something to drink, I was a stranger and you welcomed me, I was naked and you gave me clothing, I was sick and you took care of me, I was in prison and you visited me" (Matthew 25:35–36).

One of the most important contributions to pastoral care after the New Testament was by Pope Gregory I the Great. His Pastoral Care, written after he became bishop of Rome in 590, was so influential that it became customary to present it to new bishops upon their ordination. This textbook of the medieval episcopate emphasized the role of the pastor as shepherd of souls.

The medieval institutionalization of pastoral care in the sacrament of penance led to certain deficits in practice: the exclusion of the laity by emphasis upon the central role of the priest and the distortion of its original spiritual purposes of prayer, repentance, and forgiveness of sins by the introduction of paid indulgences. The indulgence abuse sparked the Reformation critique of the sacrament of penance. This in turn led to the reformers' emphasis upon lay as well as clerical responsibility for pastoral care as expressed in their teaching of "the priesthood of all believers." The Reformation insistence upon justification by grace alone shifted the burden of proof for salvation from human accomplishment to divine promise. By "letting God is God," the reformers claimed that persons were free to be human. This shift of theological focus, from an otherworldly achievement to a this-worldly trust in God, facilitated a renewed holistic awareness of human needs.

2.11. Qualities of a Pastoral Caregiver

Describe the essential qualities of a pastoral caregiver. Outline literature used to support your assumptions. Discuss the qualities you believe that you have already and what you recognize you need to develop. Include how you intend to do this.

The shepherd was with his flock day and night, often in remote places far from home, and he had to be skilled in keeping the flock together, in finding wanderers and stragglers, in recognizing the ailments of his sheep and knowing how to cure them, and in ensuring the safety of the vulnerable members of the flock.'; This definition of the role of a pastoral caregiver highlights the necessity for certain fundamental qualities within an individual in this role. These qualities include integrity, relevant response to issues of the time, deep knowledge of the heart of God, humility, and love.

Deep knowledge of the heart of God, is the most important quality for someone in a pastoral role. Do you know the incarnate God? In our world of loneliness and despair, there is an enormous need for men and women who know the heart of god, a heart that forgives, that cares, that reaches out and wants to heal… The knowledge of Jesus' heart is a knowledge of the heart. And when we live in the world with that knowledge, we cannot do other than bring healing, reconciliation, new life, and hope wherever we go.'; Spiritual maturity is essential as the above quote of Henri Nouwen explains and is further defined by St Gregory the Great where he wrote, "That man, therefore, sought by all means to be drawn with cords to be an example of good living who studies so to live that he may be able to water even dry hearts with the streams of doctrine for a rounded and biblically sound approach as a caregiver. However, the relationship between the individual and Christ is inevitably ever changing. The pastoral caregiver has to have an open mind to this spiritual development in such things as his or her spiritual gifts, for growth within him or herself and within his or her care giving.

Other Qualities of pastoral care counselors includes;

2.12. What are the qualities of a pastoral counselor?

Respect for the Counselee. The pastor-counselor will never make any counselee feel that the problem he wishes to discuss is too trivial for his attention. ...

Understanding of Himself. ...

Training. ...

Cooperation with Other Professions. ...

Security.

2.13. What is the Role of Pastoral Counseling?

Thus pastoral counseling offers a relationship to that understanding of life and faith. Pastoral counseling uses both psychological and theological resources to deepen its understanding of the pastoral relationship." Membership in several organizations that combine theology and mental health has grown in recent years.

2.14. Ten Qualities that make a Good Counsellor

Counsellors play a huge part in helping their clients to talk about their feelings, relieve distress, make positive changes in their life and understand why they are behaving in a certain way.

Encompassing a range of different specialisms, counsellors work across a wide range of settings and in lots of different sectors. Helping people resolve physiological, emotional and relationship issues, counsellors encourage people to talk about difficult, distressing or challenging times in their lives, which may be having a detrimental impact on how they function day-to-day.

Providing support for issues such as divorce, relationship breakdowns, bereavement, anxiety, depression, substance abuse and more, a counsellor will aim to get to the root of a problem while listening in an empathetic way.

Ultimately, counselling is all about forming a connection with your client that allows you to facilitate positive changes by creating a high level of trust. It can be an incredibly rewarding and worthwhile profession.

But what makes a good counsellor?

1. Communication Skills

If you are considering embarking on a career in counselling, you must have excellent communication skills, especially verbal communication. You will spend your days talking to clients about a vast range of issues and it's important that you have the skills to support, question, and encourage your patients, without judgement.

2. Empathy

A counsellor must have empathy – the ability to understand the feelings of others. You need the ability to see things from your client's perspective and understand their point of view, whether you agree with it or not.

3. Interpersonal Skills

As well as being able to express yourself clearly, you'll also need to be able to gauge your client's understanding of what you are asking them. A good counsellor will be able to sense how a client is feeling and respond appropriately. This involves showing empathy and acceptance and, ultimately, making sure that your client feels comfortable to have an open and honest conversation in your presence.

4. Trust

We are more likely to open up about how we are feeling when we trust someone.

With this in mind, you must conduct yourself in a trustworthy manner and reassure your client that you will not share anything that they tell you with others. A relationship that is built on trust will allow you to form a deeper connection with your client.

5. Awareness of Diversity

Counsellors work with clients from all cultural, ethnic, and socioeconomic backgrounds, as well as those with different expressions of gender and sexuality. It's important that you welcome and recognize this diversity, ensuring your clients feel comfortable and accepted. Treatment plans should also be created with a client's cultural values in mind, and must always show respect for their beliefs and attitudes.

6. Patience

Patience is a core skill that all counsellors need. After all, not every client will open up to you immediately and you will need to accept that progress can take time. You will need to remain positive and focused on the end goal and don't feel disheartened if it takes longer to get your client to where they need to be.

7. Self-Awareness

It's important that all counsellors can separate their personal issues from topics discussed with their clients. Counsellors are human too, and it's highly likely that, at some point in your career, your sessions will cover issues you have personal experience with.

When this happens, you need the self-awareness to manage your responses and your reactions.

8. Listening Skills

To build trust with your client, it's important that they know you understand them. This means carefully listening to their emotions and experiences, and providing non-verbal clues that you are giving them your full attention. For example, wait until the client has finished speaking; never interrupt them.

9. Self-Care

Counsellors need the ability to care for themselves, as well as others. Supporting others with their traumas, issues, and concerns, can be extremely demanding mentally. So you must be able to set personal limits and boundaries and recognize when you need to care for yourself.

10. Knowledge of Laws and Regulations

Finally, a good counsellor will always ensure that they have a sound knowledge and understanding of the laws and regulations that regulate the industry. This is incredibly important – all counsellors must demonstrate that they are able to carry out counselling sessions in line with these boundaries.

If you're thinking of becoming a counsellor, get in touch to find out how to become a counsellor or sign up for one of our Chrysalis Counsellor Courses.

Activity 2.2:

1. Analyze ten qualities of caregivers? --

----

2. Caregivers are role models. Examine the truth of this statement--------------

----

2.15. Benefits of Pastoral Counseling

Pastoral counseling may be a lovely thing for someone who is in need of help, and it will offer the client a forum to speak about their problems that makes them feel a bit more protected than they would at any other time. They may not prefer to go to a professional counselor, and the counselor who is often best is the pastor. This includes the benefits of pastoral counseling in a simplified manner.

1.The Pastor Is Confidential

The relationship between someone and their pastor is no less professional that the one they have with their therapist. The relationship is quite simple to understand as the pastor cannot share anything they hear in their sessions. They have a biblical insight into the problem, and they will offer practical solutions to the problem that are helpful for the clients or their partner. Someone who has come to pastoral counseling will receive their assistance behind closed doors where no one will know the true nature of the conversation.

2.The Church May Feel More Comfortable

There are quite a few people who are going to feel more comfortable when they are in the church, and they will feel a calm they cannot get in an office building. The pastoral relationship they have may be longstanding, and they will find it much easier to talk to this person over someone they do not know. The level of familiarity may be quite helpful as it will help the client open up about their problems, and the pastor will have practical examples to share that both parties understand.

3. Pastors Are Not Psychologists

Someone who does not wish to feel as though they are having their mind analyzed may come to the pastor, and they may speak freely to them pastor without any reservations. The two may have a conversation that remains as simple as possible, and it is difficult for either side to read too much into what has been said.

4. Pastors Are Trained to Be Comforting

Pastors work in a field where they are asked to be comforting most of the time. Their presence is to be a bit of a comfort to someone who is nervous, and the people who come to see their pastor will feel much better about the talk they are having. The talk they are enjoying will be an exciting for everyone, and they will share a connection that crosses the boundaries of the professional relationship that is found with a therapist.

5. Pastors Do Quite a Lot of Couple's Counseling

The benefits of pastoral counseling extend to couples where necessary. Someone who wishes to out issues with their spouse may come to the pastor for help as they have mediated many disputes in the past. The work they do lends itself to helping those who have marital problems, and someone who is searching for a better couple's therapist may wish to go to the church for help. The church will provide a safe space to talk, and they will ensure the couple may receive help without a battle over psychology.

The finest examples of pastoral counseling are those where clients are given help that is not forceful or psychological. The simplest solution may be the best one in many cases, and someone who is coming to their pastor for counseling will feel much better about the process simply because they are spoke to someone who understands the situation. Sidestepping a therapist may be a wise choice for someone who wishes to meet with a pastor.

Conclusion

Africa is a continent ravaged by challenges of poverty, scourge of disease and many conflicts, some of which are motivated by religious fanaticism. Indeed, it is a continent in dire need of spiritual, economic and social transformation. In the midst of these challenges, however, faith healing practices have flourished among African communities. Healing is a broad concept, which covers a whole range of social, psychological, cultural and spiritual issues and dimensions in response to unwanted threatening conditions that disturb a harmonious and peaceful existence. The concept of healing is firmly rooted in the soil and soul of Africa. To a certain extent, the popularity of healing practices in many parts of Africa is a result of an African epistemology that accepts healing as a cultural reality. The poor majority are mostly exposed to harsh socio-economic and hazardous health conditions. Thus, many poor people are drawn to healing practices for the following three reasons: Firstly, faith healers promise to heal people of all kinds of illnesses and epidemics through fervent prayers. Faith healers are powerful and charismatic personalities that command a great following as a result of their charisma. Secondly, because African culture is spirit-centered and has a high regard for spiritual powers and forces, Africans are amused by supernatural and are therefore drawn to healing phenomena, as it speaks to their reality and reference framework. Thirdly, faith healing practice is a cost free, alternative intervention strategy for managing illness, especially to the poor masses, who do not have access to specialized medical care. The close relationship between psychosomatic diseases and "African illnesses" is also explored. This is quite evident when considering the types of illnesses faith healers claim people are being healed from during healing practices, for example HIV and AIDS, hypertension, ulcers, bad luck, infertility, witchcraft, and so forth. African illnesses are believed to be unexplainable and untreatable by Western medicine. It is believed to be caused by witchcraft, sorcery and evil, and has similar manifestations as psychosomatic diseases. In the context of a vibrant and growing faith healing practice, there is a need to investigate the spiritual and emotional impact of faith healing on healing seekers, especially when the desired healing doesn't materialize. The research field has highlighted the emotional and spiritual challenges caused by illness, as well as the lack of supporting systems to sustain people grappling with illness. The realization is that healing, as a broad concept, needs a multifaceted approach for effective response. The lack of indigenization of healing practices with African (Namibian) cultural symbols and cultural milieu was highlighted. Therefore, an effective and culturally relevant pastoral care system should take special cognizance of it and thus, the envisaged pastoral approach of hope and compassion build around it.

Chapter References

1.Johnson, Patricia. "Pastoral Care." Journal of Health Care Chaplaincy 2, no. 1 (January 3, 1989): 17–31. http://dx.doi.org/10.1300/j080v02n01_03.

2.Saylor, Reverend Dennis. "Pastoral Care." JONA: The Journal of Nursing Administration 20, no. 2 (February 1990): 15. http://dx.doi.org/10.1097/00005110-199002000-00005.

3.shaffner, Julie W. "Pastoral Care." JONA: The Journal of Nursing Administration 20, no. 2 (February 1990): 16???19. http://dx.doi.org/10.1097/00005110-199002000-00006.

4.Lee, Hee Cheol. "Pastoral Care: The Future Plan of Pastoral Counseling According to Pastoral Care." Korean Journal of Christian Studies 116 (April 30, 2020): 489–514. http://dx.doi.org/10.18708/kjcs.2020.04.116.1.489.

5.Carolus Boromeus, Kusmaryanto. "HEALTH PASTORAL CARE." Jurnal Teologi 5, no. 1 (May 25, 2016): 91–104. http://dx.doi.org/10.24071/jt.v5i1.483.

6.Sunderland, Ronald D. "Lay Pastoral Care." Journal of Pastoral Care 42, no. 2 (June 1988): 159–71. http://dx.doi.org/10.1177/002234098804200207.

7. "You are a chosen race, a royal priesthood, a holy nation, God's own people, that you may declare the wonderful deeds of him who called you out of darkness into his marvelous light." I Peter 2:9 (NEB)

8.Clinebell, Howard. "Greening Pastoral Care." Journal of Pastoral Care 48, no. 3 (September 1994): 209–14. http://dx.doi.org/10.1177/002234099404800301.

9.SUNDERLAND, ROD. "WHITHER PASTORAL CARE?" Journal of Pastoral Theology 12, no. 2 (October 2002): 74–89. http://dx.doi.org/10.1179/jpt.2002.12.2.007.

10.Roberts, Margaret. "Whither Pastoral Care?" Pastoral Care in Education 24, no. 2 (June 2006): 62–64. http://dx.doi.org/10.1111/j.1468-0122.2006.00366.

11.You might also be interested in the extended bibliographies on the topic 'Pastoral care' for particular source types:

Journal articles Dissertations / Theses Books

Dissertations / Theses on the topic "Pastoral care":

12.Lister, James Kenneth. "Harmony in pastoral care music meeting pastoral care needs /." Theological Research Exchange Network (TREN), 1995. http://www.tren.com.

13.Stein, Donald M. "Pastoral care groups." Online full text .pdf document, available to Fuller patrons only, 2001. http://www.tren.com.

14.Khoaseb, Martin. "The faith healing practice in pastoral care: a pastoral assessment." Thesis, Stellenbosch: Stellenbosch University, 2014. http://hdl.handle.net/10019.1/86229.

15Thesis (PhD)--Stellenbosch University, 2014.

16.Hartman, Wilmer J. "A covenant model for pastoral care of pastoral couples." Theological Research Exchange Network (TREN), 1986. http://www.tren.com.

16.Martin, Charles C. "Rethinking pastoral care with African Americans pastoral care with African Americans amid contextual change /." Theological Research Exchange Network (TREN), 2000. http://www.tren.com.

17Yang, Yoo Sung. "Pastoral care for the dying." Theological Research Exchange Network (TREN), 1987. http://www.tren.com.

18.Mascia, Albert. "Pastoral care of the homeless." Theological Research Exchange Network (TREN), 1988. http://www.tren.com.

18.Rathgeb, William Richard. "Pastoral care of university students." Theological Research Exchange Network (TREN), 1990. http://www.tren.com.

19.Turton, Douglas W. "Pastoral care of the clergy." Thesis, Bangor University, 2003. http://ethos.bl.uk/OrderDetails.do?uin=uk.bl.ethos.401896.

21.Freville, C. Benjamin. "Pastoral care and cultural diversity." Theological Research Exchange Network (TREN), 1992. http://www.tren.com.

22.Graham, Larry Kent. Care of persons, care of worlds: A psycho-systems approach to pastoral care and counseling. Nashville: Abingdon Press, 1992.

23.John, Patton. Pastoral care in context: An introduction to pastoral care. Louisville, Ky: Westminster/John Knox Press, 1993.

24.Sharon, Reed, and Center for Youth Ministry Development., eds. Pastoral care. New Rochelle, NY: World of Don Bosco Multimedia, 1993.

25.Koenig, Harold George. Pastoral care of older adults: Creative pastoral care can be counseling. Minneapolis, MN: Fortress Press, 1998.

26.1949-, Ramsay Nancy J., ed. Pastoral care and counseling: Redefining the paradigms. Nashville, TN: Abingdon Press, 2004.

27.Ramsay, Nancy J. Pastoral care and counseling: Redefining the paradigms. Seoul: Grisim, 2012.

28.Campbell, Alastair V. Rediscovering pastoral care. 2nd ed. London: Darton, Longman & Todd, 1986.

29.Butler, Sarah A. Caring ministry: A contemplative approach to pastoral care. New York: Continuum, 1999.

30. Pattison, Stephen. A critique of pastoral care. 3rd ed. London: SCM Press, 2000.

31.Pattison, Stephen. A critique of pastoral care. 2nd ed. London: SCM Press, 1993.

32. Swanson, Robert. "Pastoral care." In Pastoral Care in Medieval England, 123–41. 1 [edition]. | New York : Routledge, 2019.: Routledge, 2019. http://dx.doi.org/10.4324/9781315599649.

33. McClure, Barbara. "Pastoral Care." In The Wiley-Blackwell Companion to Practical Theology, 267–78. Oxford, UK: Wiley-Blackwell, 2011. http://dx.doi.org/10.1002/9781444345742.ch25.

34. Walter, Tony. "Pastoral Care." In The Eclipse of Eternity, 137–48. London: Palgrave Macmillan UK, 1996. http://dx.doi.org/10.1057/9780230379770_11.

35. Sipling, William. "Fundamentalist Pastoral Care." In Encyclopedia of Psychology and Religion, 933–35. Cham: Springer International Publishing, 2020. http://dx.doi.org/10.1007/978-3-030-24348-7_200057.

36. Sipling, William. "Fundamentalist Pastoral Care." In Encyclopedia of Psychology and Religion, 1–3. Berlin, Heidelberg: Springer Berlin Heidelberg, 2018. http://dx.doi.org/10.1007/978-3-642-27771-9_200057-1.

37. Lartey, Emmanuel Y. Amugi. "Post-colonializing Pastoral Theology." In Pastoral Theology and Care, 79–97. Chichester, UK: John Wiley & Sons, Ltd, 2018. http://dx.doi.org/10.1002/9781119292586.ch4.

38. Carey, Lindsay B., and Jeffrey Cohen. "Pastoral and Spiritual Care." In Encyclopedia of Global Bioethics, 2136–48. Cham: Springer International Publishing, 2016. http://dx.doi.org/10.1007/978-3-319-09483-0_326.

39. Carey, Lindsay B., and Jeffrey Cohen. "Pastoral and Spiritual Care." In Encyclopedia of Global Bioethics, 1–14. Cham: Springer International Publishing, 2015. http://dx.doi.org/10.1007/978-3-319-05544-2_326-1.

40.Carey, Lindsay B., and Jeffrey Cohen. "Pastoral and Spiritual Care." In Encyclopedia of Global Bioethics, 1–14. Cham: Springer International Publishing, 2015. http://dx.doi.org/10.1007/978-3-319-05544-2_326-2

CHAPTER THREE

Biblical Models of Pastoral Care and Counseling

3.1. Three Pastoral Models of Pastoral Care

1. The Shepherd and the Contextual type.

2. The Wounded Healer and the Experiential type. ...

In the same way the pastor as wounded healer is motivated by love and not self-promotion.

3. The Wise Fool and the Revisionist type.

All these models of pastoral care would be discussed in this chapter.

Donald Capps very helpfully outlines models and schemata for effective pastoral action, that I think are very helpful for getting pastors to think about the what and why of what they do in a community over which they exercise pastoral oversight. This post is the third of three that will develop this scheme to show how pastoral care is multi-layered and complex, requiring self-understanding, and avoiding the over-simplification of a one-dimensional approach that can be seen in self-promoting and self-serving distortions of ministry.

In Pastoral Care and Hermeneutics (a book I discovered by reading Anthony. This Elton's a Lifetime in the Church and University), Capps first provides six Diagnostic Types for pastoral care approaches (pg. 61-65) and then, what concerned the first two posts, he locates them on three axes, with each axis viewed as a model of theological diagnosis (pg. 65-66). He uses the content analysis of published sermons in six well known preachers, showing that each preacher had a characteristic approach that was common to most if not all of their published sermons.

Now following on from the Contextual, Experiential and Revisionist models of the previous post, Capps now draws these threads together (pg. 72-78) in three characteristic models or modes of pastoral ministry (A Conceptual Schema for Interpreting Pastoral Actions), that he draws from the work of Alastair Campbell in his Rediscovering Pastoral Care:

Capps locates his three models of theological diagnosis thus: The Shepherd fits the contextual model. The wounded healer fits the experiential model. And the wise fool fits the revisionist model.

1. The Shepherd and the Contextual type. Biblically, the shepherd is one who knows the world in which the sheep live and understands the dangers they face and how to get them to safety and pasture. The shepherd does not shield them from every danger or difficulty they face, but rather, helps them to cope with them by presence, guidance and solicitous gestures. The shepherd is aware (self-aware) of the limits confronting the sheep, especially death and other serious threats. The shepherd's action is one of "tender and solicitous concern" (S. Hiltner), but without any guidance becoming coercive or paternalistic, since the goal of all pastoral care is to help people to help themselves (my emphasis). The shepherd guides without taking away freedom, even if this means making mistakes they will later regret.

The shepherd metaphor is rooted in both Old and New Testaments; Yahweh is Israel's Shepherd (Psalm 23) and Jesus is the Good Shepherd (John 10). In both senses, when the sheep are without a shepherd, they lose all sense of meaningful context. This image fits the contextual model because the shepherd is aware of the range of possible causes of discomfort, and is best equipped to discover resources to help the sheep. Additionally, the shepherd's ministry is one of a spirit of hope and confidence: "Even though I walk through the valley of the shadow of death, I fear no evil; for you are with me; your rod and your staff they comfort me" (Ps. 23:4).

2. The Wounded Healer and the Experiential type. This image is also biblical, and is primarily based on the image of the suffering Christ. The wounded healer, according to Campbell, is one who, restores the fractured relationships between God, humanity, and the whole universe. Jesus' wounds, in life and death, are the expressions of his openness to our suffering. He suffered because of his love: his sufferings are the stigmata of his care for us and for the whole would estranged from God."

The sufferings of Christ promote healing because they are the consequence of his deep love for us, and such love heals:

"Such wounded love has a healing power because it is selfless love, entering into our human weakness, feeling our pain, standing beside us in our dereliction."

In the same way the pastor as wounded healer is motivated by love and not self-promotion. The pastor must also share in sufferings, as one sharing a common humanity. While every individual is unique in their suffering, and no one can ever fully enter into that pain, we are not so different, that no communication, no reverberation of feelings is impossible. This does mean that on some level, which must be found, pain is sharable and we can, in this way, know and understand the sufferings of another. Those who would deny all possible pastoral help because "you don't know what I'm suffering" are claiming a uniqueness to their own being that is simply not there, nor is it theirs to claim.

Obviously, the goal of the wounded healer is to see healing. But this model insists that healing does not come by isolating or distancing ourselves from painful experience (if that were possible), or even "working through" our pain, but by living our pain, allowing ourselves to experience it fully. Henri Nouwen reminds us in his Wounded Healer, "A minister is not a doctor whose primary task is to take away pain. Rather he deepens the pain to a level where it can be shared."

This means that for effective pastoral ministry, the minister helps others to reject the false supposition that life should be painless, free from fear, despair, loneliness, and estrangement. Indeed, those who avoid life's pain (if they can) are ultimately poorer for it, because as we live our pain fully we also experience the unrelenting love of God and the peace that passes all understanding.

The wounded healer has the same concern for the suffering of others that we saw in the shepherd but does not address this concern by seeking to mobilize the available resources for alleviating pain. Instead, the wounded healer encourages us to live our pain as deeply as we are able, to drink the bitter cup down to its very dregs. While the shepherd holds out hope to the threatened sheep, the wounded healer puts stress on the power of God's love whatever may happen. Both models envision victory over the powers of sickness and death; one on victory over the dangers, the other on the abiding presence of God whose love knows no limits: "If I go to the depths of Sheol, you are there" (Ps. 139:8b).

3. The Wise Fool and the Revisionist type. The "wise fool" (coined by Campbell) is a pastoral image whereby the pastor functions much like a clown in a circus – hospital chaplaincy fits this model very well. Like the other two models, this is also biblical, in that we are not be wise in our own eyes, but become a fool (1 Cor. 3:18). On this basis, the pastor is neither worldly wise nor "just a fool," but an apparent fool who is in fact a person of wisdom. (This reminds me of a book by Rev'd Dr Helen Paynter called 'Reduced Laughter' which I reviewed here, and develops the Wise Fool as a hermeneutical model using the middle section of the Books of 1 & 2 Kings). In any case, there are three main characteristics of the wise fool:

-Simplicity. Seen in a refreshing directness and refusal to play language games that jockey for position and power.

- Loyalty. Seen in an undramatic but persistent loyalty to others in disregard of self.

- Prophecy. Seen in the tendency to challenge accepted norms, conventions and authorities within society.

Adopting this self-understanding always runs the risk of being thought unorthodox by fellow ministers, but it may also command a certain deep-seated respect for daring to challenge the empty professionalism and self-promotion in much contemporary ministry. Pastors who function as the Wise Fool are often underestimated and taken for granted, being dismissed to easily, with ideas deemed unrealistic or unworthy of serious consideration.

The wise fool helps us "to see ourselves in a clearer light."

Through prophecy the wise fool helps us to see what our social institutions are doing to us.

Through simplicity, the challenge is to conduct our professional lives with less self-serving distortion.

Through loyalty, the wise fool challenges us to be more truthful in our interpersonal relationships.

In this way, the wise fool fits the revisionist model because we are encouraged to look at life in new ways, and this because we have preferred darkness to light and truth. The wise fool helps us see that "Truth is remarkably simple; error is unnecessarily complex." Professional and personal relationships can be remarkably straightforward and clear if we do not insist on deceiving one another, but instead relate to each other with the same honesty and straightforwardness with which God relates to us.

In this model, what we formerly considered foolishness is now wisdom, and our former wisdom is now folly. Such reversals reveal a new world to us, one to which we had previously been blind or impervious.

3.2. Synoptic Gospels Models of pastoral care and counseling

In John 10:1-24, Jesus teaches us on how to care for the flocks. Pay careful attention to yourselves and to all the flock, in which the Holy Spirit has made you overseers, to care for the church of God, which he obtained with his own.

Ministry is not something that is weird to every Christian because it is a Christian lifestyle that was exemplified by Jesus Himself when He served three and a half years on earth because basically service is an activity carried out by someone to help others in meeting the needs of that person. Jesus specifically said in Matthew 20:28 "just as the Son of Man did not come to be served, but to serve and to give His life as a ransom for many. "Herlianto in the book Urban Ministry states that: As a ministry that includes preaching the good gospel verbally and in action and is aimed at reaching out to the whole human being as well, namely humans consisting of body, soul and spirit, and humans who have social, cultural, economic, legal and political links to their environment. Tomatala (2002) said: about the nature of a holistic ministry which can be described as a "whole one" which has an integral unity with complete aspects. Services that touch basic ministry aspects in four holistic ministry dimensions, namely spiritual, psychological, social and physical human beings. For this reason, it has become an obligation and necessity for Christians and even churches to implement holistic ministry that are not only focused on "people oriented" or caring for people but how one can live ideally as God's creation. The church is in charge of educating children until one day they reach a mature faith and pay attention to their needs by providing holistic service. Especially or children aged 14 to 19 years, because that is the age where children begin to grow from teenagers to adults and are ready to grow into spiritual leaders. At the same time – a period of risk because the child enters the puberty phase where the emotional tendency is more unstable. The period of adolescent development is also the stage of puberty.

The stage of puberty (puberty) is a period in which physical maturity takes place rapidly, which involves hormonal and bodily changes, which mainly take place in early adolescence. Therefore, the author describes the holistic ministry in the synoptic gospels in this writing in order to provide an understanding for believers to bring youth and youth to become people who love God.

The Bible is the content of God's heart that is poured out in writing to humans with the aim that humans can understand and understand correctly about God's care and love that never ends in human life. In the Gospel of Matthew, Mark and Luke are referred to as the Synoptic Gospels because they are known for the element of similarity in the stories written in the three Gospels. There are only three gospels called the Synoptic Gospels, namely: Matthew, Mark, and Luke. For this reason, the author pours Holistic Ministry based on the Synoptic Gospels among Youth and Youth Service. What is recorded in the study of theory in holistic ministry in the synoptic book.

3.3 The Essentials of Holistic Ministry

Ministry can basically be defined as the activities of a person, group, or organization either directly or indirectly to meet needs. Ministry is the process of meeting needs through the activities of others directly. Moreover, the responsibility to serve is not only entrusted to special people such as pastors, elders, or deacons, but starts from the congregation who are called to serve because of their faith in God and their response to becoming a Christian. The basis of the first ministry is the initiative of God, God who works and dirty His hands to create (serve humans). Then God gave orders to humans to cultivate the garden and take care of it, God was giving orders to humans to serve God through His commands. Thus service is the command and will of God. In this command, God is also present and with humans. The glory of God radiates through man.

Service is not just an order, but there is also an intimate relationship between humans and God. While the word 'holistic' comes from the word "whole"

(English) which means: whole, completely of an organism". The term holistic ministry is currently widely used by various groups to indicate the form of service, but there are also groups of people who misinterpret it. There is often a misunderstanding about holistic ministry is the assumption that holistic ministries are services in the form of social services, so that in the end there are those who mean that holistic ministries are social services. The understanding of a holistic ministry is as a ministry that includes preaching the gospel both verbally and in action and is aimed at reaching the whole human being as well, namely humans consisting of body, soul and spirit, and humans who have social, cultural, economic, law and politics with the environment [1, p. 123]. Holistic ministry which includes service elements: Koinonia (fellowship), Martyria (witness), and Diakonia (social service), is an absolute thing that underlines evangelism and brings shalom (peace, salvation) promised by God [9, p. 45]. A holistic ministry which can be described as a "whole one" which has an integral unity with complete aspects. Evangelism touches basic ministry aspects in four holistic ministry dimensions, namely: Fellowship (koinoneo), Ministry (diakoneo),

Testimony (martureo) and Preaching (kerigma/kerusso). Holistic ministry aims at the welfare of the whole human being, meaning to preach the full gospel to a whole human being in various dimensions. Therefore, holistic ministry must pay attention to all of these dimensions, namely spiritual, psychological and physical human beings. Holistic ministry seeks to restore balance and harmony between the individual and social dimensions of human beings.

Therefore, in holistic ministry, there is no dichotomy or separation between individual and social human needs.

3.4. The Essential of Contemporary Youth Generation

Adolescence is a period of transition or transition from childhood to adulthood. The period in which individuals in the process of growth (especially physical growth) have reached maturity, they no longer want to be treated as children, but they have not reached full maturity and have not entered the stage of adult development. Negatively, this period is also called the "unbalanced" or unbalanced, unstable, and unpredictable period. In this period there were changes both in terms of psychological, social and intellectual. Adolescence or ages 12–22 is a period of transition between childhood and adulthood. During this period of development, adolescents reach physical, mental, social and emotional maturity [11, p. 12]. Several studies on physical growth in adolescents show that height growth in adolescence is faster than in previous periods, and changes in body proportions in female adolescents occur more rapidly than in male adolescents. 12, 13 or 14 year girls are taller than boys [12, p. 66]. The period of adolescent development is also the stage of puberty. The stage of puberty (puberty) is a period in which physical maturity takes place rapidly, which involves hormonal and bodily changes, which mainly take place in early adolescence.

Adolescents in the stages of cognitive development enter the formal operational stage. This formal operational stage is experienced by children aged 11 years and over. At this formal operational stage, the child has been able to realize a whole in his work which is the result of logical thinking. The emotional and moral aspects have also developed.". According to Piaget, in this stage adolescents begin to interact with the environment and are wider than the stages of children, adolescents begin to interact with their peers and even try to be able to interact with adults. Because at this stage, children have begun to be able to develop their normal thoughts, they are also able to achieve logic and reason and can use abstraction. They can understand the symbolic and figurative meaning. Involving them in an activity will have a more positive impact on their cognitive development. Therefore, a mentor is required to be pro-active, creative and innovative in directing youth.

In Luke 4:14-30, Jesus revealed Himself in fulfilling the prophecy of Elijah and Elisha and being the Savior of the marginalized. The calling of the pastoral caregiver is to be the hands and feet of Jesus, especially to the marginalized. Jesus also brought reconciliation and spiritual transformation to the person in need. Luke portrays Jesus as the anointed one through the Spirit. Three keys provide access to the understanding of the passages in Luke, of which the first is exegeses of the passages themselves and in historical context. Secondly, interactive internalization provides the reader of the passages with the opportunity to focus on the Word and Spirit and to internalize the event.

Thirdly, through the process of appropriation, spiritual growth and transformation takes place.

The article aims at deducing from Luke 4:14-30 guidelines concerning reconciliation (as imperative in pastoral care) for the pastoral caregiver. In this periscope, Jesus focuses on the marginalized (the poor/suppressed/outcasts) and wants to bring reconciliation through the Spirit. According to Bezuidenhout (2005:3), pastoral care can be defined as the ministry of reconciliation in accordance with 2 Corinthians 5:19-20, namely "that God was reconciling the world to himself in Christ, not counting men's sins against them. And he has committed to us the message of reconciliation. We are therefore Christ's ambassadors, as though God were making his appeal through us. We implore you on Christ's behalf: Be reconciled to God".

However, a ministry of reconciliation cannot be practiced without taking into consideration the covenant between God and humankind. In our view, Johan Janse van Rensburg's research on the "covenant as proprium" in pastoral care is his most dynamic contribution, if one has to single out something.

According to Janse van Rensburg (1996:152-153), the covenant as "the most important Biblical foundational motive" offers an "excellently fitting and all-inclusive proprium for poimenics as science and pastoral care as a strategy of ministry" (own translation). By making use of a comparative analysis and interpretation of literature on the topic, Janse van Rensburg came to the conclusion that, from a Biblical and theological perspective, the covenant is appropriate as a proprium for a reformed theory of pastoral care.

The covenant presupposes and includes all other foundational motives that should be found in pastoral care, i.e. the Council of God, the kingdom, kerugma and change, koinonia, bipolarity and the power of binding and releasing eschatology, soteriology and pneumatology. However, the covenant does not figure sufficiently in the practice of pastoral care.

If one were to accept that the task of the pastoral caregiver entails the reconciliation of man in need with God, one cannot but ask: What is the contribution of Luke 4:14-30 to the meaning of the new covenant God has concluded with man in Jesus Christ, and what are its implications for pastoral care? Methodologically, this article also touches on the question of the use of the covenant in pastoral care, because Luke 4:14-30 is used to deduce guidelines for the pastoral care of the marginalized. The work of Senekal (2005) concerning the "functioning of the Biblical contents in a narrative-pastoral discussion" (own translation) offers a useful grounding of the use of the Bible in pastoral counselling, especially for the pastoral narrative approach and thus also for the methodology of the current article. The history of the movement for pastoral care in South Africa and abroad indicates that there have been/are proponents who view the use of the Bible in pastoral care as essential, but there are also clear voices warning against the legalistic and prescriptive use of the Bible in pastoral care (Senekal 2005:78). Still in the foreground is the search for principles that could guide the use of the Bible.

The principles Capps (1990:82-83) formulated twenty years ago could still be regarded as providing direction:

• Whatever use is made of the Bible in pastoral care, it should be guided by the particular needs and circumstances of the patient.

• Its use should reflect pastoral sensitivity to the patient's acute or chronic physical and psychological limitations.

- Whatever use is made of the Bible in pastoral care or counselling, it should be consistent with the counselling principles and method that inform the pastoral intervention as a whole.

- Once we recognize that the dynamic power of a Bible text is its capacity to disclose a world, we can also see how the Bible (as a whole) may play a more decisive role in pastoral care.

In this article, the hermeneutic use of the Bible to deduce principles for pastoral care is supported. As such, the Bible does not provide direct and simple answers to the questions and problems of life that one encounters in the pastoral situation. Heitink (1998:80) determined that pastoral care has moved from a kerygmatic and a therapeutic phase to a hermeneutic phase such as "understanding, insight, meaning, construal and interpretation" of Scripture. In this process, the "narrative, language, predisposition, context and epistemological approach will strongly influence the process of understanding" (Bezuidenhout & Janse van Rensburg 2006:19, own translation).

According to Louw (2000:225-25), a hermeneutic process offers the pastor the opportunity to connect the narrative of salvation (reconciliation) to the struggle, suffering, heartache and joy of the marginalized. In reality, it connects the kerygmatic and hermeneutic processes to one another. One of the unique aims of the pastor should be to change an inappropriate, obstructive and negative image of God, which inhibits the process of developing faith and a relationship with God, into an image of a God who is present - full of love and compassionate - in times of need Senekal (2005:78) indicates that the question concerning the "dynamic power of the Bible text itself" (own translation) is currently being asked again in pastoral care. According to him, the question pertains to the "disclosing power of the text" (own translation).

Thus, the power of the Bible as God's revealed Word is central to pastoral care and this article. Amongst others, the article wishes to indicate from Luke 4:14-30 how the Biblical text is successful in creating spiritual growth in the person by means of experience and transformation.

The method of exegesis, the analysis of the cultural-historical background, interactive internalizing and pastoral development (where a pastor/caregiver may be seen as one who is serving under the power of the Holy Spirit and he/she is called to preach, teach, heal and to set the captives free) will be used to indicate what the meaning of Luke 4:14-30 is for pastoral care.

In pastoral care, the Bible is used in such a way that one has to read Luke 4:14-30 in the context of the whole of the gospel of Luke. The voice of Luke in his gospel, the reader's interpretation of the text and the complete story of Jesus form part of a revelatory understanding and a dynamic power that is released to renew an old covenant when God's promises, as written down by the prophet Isaiah, are fulfilled. Thus, in pastoral care, one cannot afford a one-sided view by considering only the story of Jesus in Nazareth, because it would imply that the cultural-historical connections of Jesus' life and His story are causing the demise of the covenant as program. In this respect, we are satisfying Capps's (1990:83) last pronouncement, as indicated above, i.e. that one has to look at the essential themes of Scripture that are connected to this periscope like, amongst others, the identity of Christ as (also) revealed in/through the cross, resurrection, ascension and the outpouring of the Holy Spirit (the new covenant). The promise of reconciliation is of the essence for pastoral care and embodies the hope of humankind in need.

Activity 3.1

1. Explain the fact that biblical models of care are holistic and holistic? --------

----

----

2. Explain that synoptic gospels models of care are empathetic? -----------------

----

3.5. Pauline Theology of Pastoral Care and Counseling

1. Acts 20:28

Pay careful attention to yourselves and to all the flock, in which the Holy Spirit has made you overseers, to care for the church of God, which he obtained with his own blood.

2. Romans 12:4–21

For as in one body we have many members, and the members do not all have the same function, so we, though many, are one body in Christ, and individually members one of another. Having gifts that differ according to the grace given to us, let us use them: if prophecy, in proportion to our faith; if service, in our serving; the one who teaches, in his teaching; the one who exhorts, in his exhortation; the one who contributes, in generosity; the one who leads, with zeal; the one who does acts of mercy, with cheerfulness.

Let love be genuine. Abhor what is evil; hold fast to what is good. Love one another with brotherly affection. Outdo one another in showing honor. Do not be slothful in zeal, be fervent in spirit, serve the Lord. Rejoice in hope, be patient in tribulation, be constant in prayer. Contribute to the needs of the saints and seek to show hospitality.

Bless those who persecute you; bless and do not curse them. Rejoice with those who rejoice, weep with those who weep. Live in harmony with one another. Do not be haughty, but associate with the lowly. Never be wise in your own sight. Repay no one evil for evil, but give thought to do what is honorable in the sight of all. If possible, so far as it depends on you, live peaceably with all. Beloved, never avenge yourselves, but leave it to the wrath of God, for it is written, "Vengeance is mine, I will repay, says the Lord." To the contrary, "if your enemy is hungry, feed him; if he is thirsty, give him something to drink; for by so doing you will help burning coals on his head." Do not be overcome by evil, but overcome evil with good.

3. 1 Peter 5:1–4

So I exhort the elders among you, as a fellow elder and a witness of the sufferings of Christ, as well as a partaker in the glory that is going to be revealed: shepherd the flock of God that is among you, exercising oversight, not under compulsion, but willingly, as God would have you; not for shameful gain, but eagerly; not domineering over those in your charge, but being examples to the flock. And when the chief Shepherd appears, you will receive the unfading crown of glory.

4. 2 Timothy 2:15

Do your best to present yourself to God as one approved, a worker who has no need to be ashamed, rightly handling the word of truth.

5. Titus 1:5–9

This is why I left you in Crete, so that you might put what remained into order, and appoint elders in every town as I directed you—if anyone is above reproach, the husband of one wife, and his children are believers and not open to the charge of debauchery or insubordination. For an overseer, as God's steward, must be above reproach. He must not be arrogant or quick-tempered or a drunkard or violent or greedy for gain, but hospitable, a lover of good, self-controlled, upright, holy, and disciplined. He must hold firm to the trustworthy word as taught, so that he may be able to give instruction in sound doctrine and also to rebuke those who contradict it.

6. Hebrews 13:7

Remember your leaders, those who spoke to you the word of God. Consider the outcome of their way of life, and imitate their faith.

7. 2 Timothy 4:2

Preach the word; be ready in season and out of season; reprove, rebuke, and exhort, with complete patience and teaching.

8. Ephesians 4:11–12

And he gave the apostles, the prophets, the evangelists, the shepherds and teachers, to equip the saints for the work of ministry, for building up the body of Christ.

9. 1 Timothy 3:1–13

The saying is trustworthy: If anyone aspires to the office of overseer, he desires a noble task. Therefore, an overseer must be above reproach, the husband of one wife, sober-minded, self-controlled, respectable, hospitable, able to teach, not a drunkard, not violent but gentle, not quarrelsome, not a lover of money.

He must manage his own household well, with all dignity keeping his children submissive, for if someone does not know how to manage his own household, how will he care for God's church? He must not be a recent convert, or he may become puffed up with conceit and fall into the condemnation of the devil. Moreover, he must be well thought of by outsiders, so that he may not fall into disgrace, into a snare of the devil.

Deacons likewise must be dignified, not double-tongued, not addicted to much wine, not greedy for dishonest gain. They must hold the mystery of the faith with a clear conscience. And let them also be tested first; then let them serve as deacons if they prove themselves blameless. Their wives likewise must be dignified, not slanderers, but sober-minded, faithful in all things. Let deacons each be the husband of one wife, managing their children and their own households well. For those who serve well as deacons gain a good standing for themselves and also great confidence in the faith that is in Christ Jesus.

Conclusion

A Comprehensive model of pastoral care is evidently demonstrated by Jesus Christ himself, and the apostles and disciples of the early Jerusalem church. The heart of caregivers from biblical perspectives, offers teaching, provides guidance, represents his clients, offers hope, and love. Jesus caregiving behavior was full of compassion to the poor, the needy, the widows and the orphans. Jesus recommended caregivers to love- love your neighbor as yourself. Apostle Paul complemented it all; love is humble and not proud, love forgives, love is not envious, love is not boastful. If caregivers must create impact, we must model our behaviors to think like Christ. Caregivers are servant leaders. A servant leader goes to the people, makes himself available, sacrifices willingly and stay with them.

www.ingramcontent.com/pod-product-compliance
Lightning Source LLC
Chambersburg PA
CBHW070939160426
43193CB00011B/1742